ROTARY

To Tisha
Thank You
Chris! 2004

ROTARY

Poems by Christina Pugh

Word Press

Published by Word Press
P.O. Box 541106
Cincinnati, OH 45254-1106

Typeset in Gill Sans and Baskerville by WordTech Communications,
Cincinnati, OH

ISBN: 1932339345
LCCN: 2003113605

Poetry Editor: Kevin Walzer
Business Editor: Lori Jareo

Visit us on the web at www.word-press.com

Cover photo: Keith Krisa
Author photo: Richard DelVisco

ACKNOWLEDGMENTS

Grateful acknowledgment is made to the editors of the following publications, in which some of these poems first appeared:

The Atlantic Monthly: "Mourning Cloak."

Beacon Street Review: "Amaryllis"; "The Blind Poem."

Columbia: A Journal of Literature and Art: "Lady's Slipper."

Ekphrasis: "The Annunciation, Attributed to Petrus Christus"; "Rest"; "Blue" (as "Picasso's Blue"); "When: On a Painting by Catherine McCarthy."

Grolier Poetry Prize Annual: "Crown"; "Savior"; "Enceinte"; "*The Watercolors of John Singer Sargent: A Catalogue.*"

Harpur Palate: "Miniature"; "Outside Boston."

Harvard Review: "Apostrophe."

Hayden's Ferry Review: "Rotary."

In Posse Review: "Background: Mark Rothko."

Isle Review: "Hydrangea."

Mystic River Review: "Book of Days."

Provincetown Arts: "Great Lakes."

Smartish Pace: "First in Flight"; "On Paternity."

Tar River Poetry: "Cherry Mary."

Third Coast: "Church Street"; "Lesson."

"Rotary" received the Associated Writing Programs' Intro Award in 2000. It was also featured on the website *Poetry Daily* (www.poems.com) on May 19, 2001, and on the website *Poetry 180: A Poem A Day for American High Schools* (www.loc.gov/poetry/180), selected by Billy Collins and sponsored by the Library of Congress. "Rotary" also appears in *Poetry 180: A Turning Back to Poetry,* edited by Billy Collins (Random House, 2003).

"Crown," "Savior," "Enceinte," and *"The Watercolors of John Singer Sargent: A Catalogue"* received the Grolier Poetry Prize for 2000.

Some of these poems appear in the chapbook *Gardening at Dusk* (Wells College Press, 2002).

I would like to thank *Poetry* magazine for a Ruth Lilly Poetry Fellowship for 2000, and the Wesleyan Writers Conference for a William Meredith Scholarship in 2003. Many thanks also to Jonathan Aaron, Gail Mazur, John Skoyles, David Barber, Sam Cornish, Robert Levine, and Reg Gibbons; to Kevin Walzer and Lori Jareo of Word Press; and to Richard DelVisco, Walter and Sybil Pugh, and Lisa Petrie. And finally, my sincere thanks to Bruce Bennett for his untiring support of this work over the last several years.

To Richard DelVisco

and to my parents

TABLE OF CONTENTS

III.

rotary, 1. turning or capable of turning around an axis, as a wheel. 2. taking place around an axis, as motion. 3. having a part or parts that turn around an axis, as a machine.

—*Webster's Encyclopedic Unabridged Dictionary*

I.

Irene is a name for a city in the distance, and if you approach, it changes.

—Italo Calvino

CHURCH STREET

Like a market with no wares,
this street of song greets you every morning:
an avenue of appeals and half-told stories.
So which palm or paper cup

will get your windfall of change
from buying newspapers and milk?
You can't judge who's neediest or coldest
on winter days when the voices are the loudest—

Help a hungry epileptic, help a hungry epileptic—
but this repeated *epileptic* wakes your inner ear,
its second beat alternating half-tones
on the chromatic scale: perfect pitch.

Hello, ma'am. I live in a homeless shelter,
and I need to get a few dollars together
for a bite to eat. Can you help me out?
The voice of an orator, groomed for the podium,

Ciceronian. Sometimes I almost feel
my tailbone scrape a sidewalk's crack at sunrise:
pitched from the lean-to of furnished life,
chanting like Lear's unaccomodated man—

Spare change, sir, ma'am, please?
Enjoy your day—or silent as the man
at the corner grocery store, his eyes closed to the sun,
his palm curved for a shower of silver.

ROSE CITY

The bleared petals
in my failed photographs

bloom again in the streets
that become, this time

each year, a city of roses.
From railings, over trellises,

I'm offered cup after cup
of blank: well-bottom colonies,

foil to the sharpened mum
or the black-eyed Susan.

Like holes, the roses
won't articulate,

resisting me
just as they resisted

the camera's perspicacity,
its tiny window trained

on overflow.
I can hear them

tear at the earth's precision:
quicksand, blind road,

the siren sheen
of the magnifying glass.

ROTARY

Closer to a bell than a bird,
that clapper ringing
the clear name
of its inventor:

by turns louder
and quieter than a clock,
its numbered face
was more literate,

triplets of alphabet
like grace notes
above each digit.

And when you dialed,
each number was a shallow hole
your finger dragged
to the silver
comma-boundary,

then the sound of the hole
traveling back
to its proper place
on the circle.

You had to wait for its return.
You had to wait.
Even if you were angry
and your finger flew,

you had to watch
the round trip
of seven holes
before you could speak.

The rotary was wired for lag,
for the afterthought.

Before the touch-tone,
before the speed-dial,
before the primal grip
of the cellular,

they built glass houses
around telephones—
glass houses in parking lots,
by the roadside,
on sidewalks.

When you stepped in
and closed the door,
transparency hugged you,
and you could almost see

your own lips move,
the dumb-show
of your new secrecy.

Why did no one think
to conserve the peal?

Just try once
to sing it to yourself:
it's gone,

like the sound of breath
if your body left.

FIRST IN FLIGHT

You thought you'd lost that old dress
years ago in a moving truck
or left it for the Salvation Army;

you thought it went the way
of turquoise eye shadow,
bell bottoms, a platinum fall—

but here are the Wright Brothers
silhouetted in polyester,
floating in folds beneath the bodice,

and fresh from Orville's wind tunnels,
their scarecrow of a plane—
all straw joints and no muscle,

once grounded at Kitty Hawk
after four low-sighing flights,
the porous warp of its wing in tatters.

Unfold them. Do you remember 1973?
Drape yourself in the faded sheath
and raise a phantom wine glass

to the eaves: now Orville's face
balloons in triumph, twelve
long seconds in the air—

now Wilbur's nose punctuates
the curve of your left knee
in *contrapposto*. Again you're beautiful

as the heights they imagined,
the galaxies they'd have gathered up
like marbles in their pockets:

two heads aloft for hours
in the region of sky
stretched from your breast

to your ankles, their shared name
looped in cirrus ink, and somewhere an aircraft
roars and hums in your wake.

CHERRY MARY

Cherry Mary (Mary Ann Fairland) was her name because
she lived on Cherry Street and was a cherry when I met her.
That condition didn't last long.
> —Neal Cassady to Jack Kerouac, Dec. 17, 1950

After he left,
she sat in the dark
and said his name to herself,
made it a mantra,
a manner of sleeping
awake, though she wouldn't
have used those words
herself: she'd just say
Neal, Neal,
savoring the way
her tongue curled up
on her palate
to initiate the *N,*
the way her lips
released the longest
vowel, a ridden *e*
before the tongue's reluctant
recurling to *l...*

it's too much to say
that the name
she spoke to herself
was like a deep inner kiss,
or that great sex
taught her
to love words:
that's never enough
to make a girl a poet,
even if her name rhymes—
as Mary's suddenly did
when Neal wrote to Jack,
telling what he took

from her, what
he kept on taking
as he ran those tracks,
her blonde body
unfurling again, relentless
as home movies.

READER

Your face is pointed like Hepburn's;
you lower your eyes.

You walk alone on a dirt road at dusk
or pause in the beam
of a traffic light.

Two hours at a movie, and you retain
a single frame:
gold dust kicked up in a barn
or a sea-feathered hat
in a window.

You speak my languages
but long for the others:
Hebrew, German,
Portuguese.

When my ignorance is a wound,
you kneel to swab it.

One winter afternoon,
you paused at Levin's wedding.
You rolled over,
and the book cradled your head.

It pressed your cheek as you slept.

FORT WORTH

Cleaned of pore and freckle,
her face lit the local
front page: cow-town Garbo,
my mother at twenty-two.

Above her pencilled brows,
a swath of hair
crafts an acanthus leaf.

Her lipstick calibrates
celluloid degrees of black
as two pearl strands
milk her neck.

*She loves pretty clothes
and animals. And people.
Especially people.*

The caption ignores the book
tucked under her arm,
its leathered edges
crumbling to cloud-stuff.

Maybe the reporter didn't know
the pick-up line,
What are you reading?

But she didn't volunteer
that information either:

it was 1959
in the City of Pretty Girls,
and she chose
to clothe the book in taffeta.

MAILLOT

She wandered on the beach that was amber then,
the prandial light of a Cold War ballet

that mapped the stage in real sand.
And her thighs swelled in her navy suit:

a sudden width, cloudlike, desultory as whiskey
on the rocks, in the years before whip

and sculpt and muscle, the hours at the gym
with the Walkmen on: can you hear the hidden music

faintly clambering? Her arms lifted
to divide the sky. She might have heard

seagulls, guitar chords from a distant radio,
and balanced for an instant there at the tip

of the known world, all its limits
shimmering, before she folded herself in,

pressed a knotted seashell to her ear.
Watched him from the corner

of her eye. And he had to find
her wide legs tender, devilishly sweet.

SOUTH BEND

Just when I've nearly learned to lull
the second vowel sound in *Louisville*
the way the TV anchors do,

I'm leaving in a taxi,
finally glimpsing more than the chains
linking Kentucky to the Great Lakes

and to New York again—
between the Gap and *Au Bon Pain*,
behind the corner Borders

are other stores my whirlwind visit missed:
Tiffany's Lounge, graced by a neon
hourglass girl; the Priddy Window Shop,

and a Winn Dixie I could whistle in,
my arms around a paper bag of corn
and collard greens. I never heard

the bluegrass, or slopped through mud
to smell the horses on their farms.
I stood behind a podium

and looked at strangers just like me
or my father, nights he flew in
from the board rooms of South Bend—

beat and stubbled, speaking one word
at a time, the cloth of his raincoat
rough to my wary hands.

ON JACKIE EARLE HALEY

Breaking Away, 1979

Growing up,
I knew ten of him:
the pothead burn-out,
Jackie with his clap
of muscle, stately
in sneakers
and torn Chinos,
a pimple low
on his jaw...
how right he was
in his skin. You can't
act that: the anchor
sunk behind the spine,
the blink underwater
when the drought's gone,
the parking lot
buffered to a flare—

so Jackie walks
to the town hall
and marries at eighteen;
he sleeps sleeveless
on the quarry rock,
barely turns his head
when the biking
trophy's won.
The dust is swirling
in my eyes,
but I can still smell
the salt in his hair.
I blink, then
I'm whispering,
I knew you. Extinct.

SAY YOU LOVE ME

The year I was ten, I thought I heard
melodic bodies of evidence.

So when my radio sang,
You woo me until the sun comes up
and you say that you love me,

I knew *woo* was the wrong word,
more suited to minuet
than the sunrise-shift
of the singer's exhaustion;
I knew her hair
was white beneath the gold,
her body lit like a coal mine,
slick with use—

but what do we ever learn
first-hand? There's a canon of hands
waving which way the wind blows,
an element fleet as helium;
so even untouched, we are never
virginal: the stain filters
through another dusky glass,

the opening bars
inflate us like breath,
and we have to glean from the sung
the unsung: no U-turn
to a life unmined;
the songbird twirls
and rusts on a barn roof.

LESSON

I learned the laws of new math
the year I read
a story called
Mysterious Wisteria.

I'd never seen wisteria,
didn't know
its wistful
cataracts;

but I let the name
whistle through me,
hollowing
what it would.

So repeat after me:
Venn diagram.
Hunker
in that consonantal cave.

Now take a pencil and paper.
Loop a large oval
on another.

See the overlap?

Shhh…
it's the interset.
Crossed curves,
a shared slice of nil.

No spores, no mouth,
no nipple.

But let your body
yearn for a moment—

you might hear
the ovals' astral hum,
the dim appeal of the air:

blueprints
for root gnarl,
a sky grid of sea—
form before our breathing forms:

smoke rings for Frost;
for Plato, wings.

BACKGROUND:
MARK ROTHKO

1.

At first there were subways and satyrs,
curving stairs or a violet dress.

He painted his own eyes
behind dark glasses,
his beard clouding a totem pole.

But blocks of color
floated behind the figures,
soon gathering opulence
and a voice:
the call of background,
a bitter call.

He was barely forty,
and on this side of the Atlantic,
the world still brimmed
with faces
and buildings he could render.

But background
murmured on the radio.
It honked in Manhattan traffic
and whispered in his ear as he slept.

2.

In 1946, Rothko sat in his studio
and held background in his hands.
He turned it over,
tracked it like an eight ball,
laid it in molecules
under the microscope.

He glimpsed the outline
of a rectangle,
then frayed its corners,
loosening colors:
red or brown or black.

I will say without reservations
that from my view there can be no abstractions,
he said.

And though there are no
right angles in nature,
his paintings shared darkness
with the larger stars,
the comet that stays in the sky
night after clear night.

3.

Brooklyn College in the fifties.
Rothko in a parka
zipped to his chin, smoking
and pacing the sidewalk,
tapping ashes
to a street packed in dirty snow:
a hell of an instructor.

He'd roll his eyes,
refuse to demonstrate.

My idea of a school
is Plato's academy, where a man learns
by conversing with men of consequence.

During breaks, he never fraternized
with the faculty.

4.

Here is the hope
that yellow gives to blue
and to that mottled strip
of white below: forms torn
from a world we've never seen
but know. How it shines—
your own heart,
stripped of its anatomy.

5.

Imagine the scarred floor of the moon
on a TV screen in Rothko's living room.
That's when the lights went out.
Blocks flat beneath his brush,
the black square
unable to kindle—
laid on white,
it was mum as newsprint.

6.

At the National Gallery retrospective,
I lingered at the hazy oils,
his cumulous islands
of bright on bright.

But in the corner, there:
two ink rectangles,
squiggled as if by a child.

He'd drawn them at sixty-five,
after an aneurysm
left him too weak
to hold a brush.

Two tiny rectangles in ink—
one hand undiminished,
groping toward the absolute:

there can be no abstractions.

OUTSIDE BOSTON

After a long sabbatical,
the sun glasses the street
again: the neighbors'
bone siding evanesces;
a clamped tulip
lightens its striated load,
and narcissus grazes a well
in the corner park.

Even the bus driver's bark—
You got a lot o' nerve,
parking there –
flutes infinitesimally,
risen from a shock
of greener world.

The sun was studying
pearling—how to skim
opacity from liquid limbs,
to amplify the unforeseen:
so the old nurse
two houses down,
veteran of ten thousand lakes,
wakes today to find herself
mayor of her town.

"What do you know,"
she says, rubbing her eyes.
Outside the window,
an entourage
rings her ancient
station wagon.

II.

I cannot reproduce the Winter Garden photograph. It exists only for me.

—Roland Barthes

APOSTROPHE

Early spring forsythia: the flowering
of the rod; wood resurrected in petals

unrelieved by leaves. Occasionally
I still mishear its name, *forsythia*,

for Cynthia, a girl given the regal
gift of yellow. The first blonde.

And when the April ice cream comes,
and men walk in shirtsleeves at noon

or stoop on weathered porches late at night...
how easy it is to speak as if you listened!

As if some local blossoming
might lure you back to this hemisphere;

but apostrophe's the supreme fiction,
as we learned. And I'd say anything.

GARDENING AT DUSK

My friend scans a low horizon,
dirt corners under a sky
darkening the recursive folds of roses,

each a thousand nights and a night,
climbing a hand's-breadth over daisies
and thistle. At the end of a dry day,

it's the rainy hour: time for mothers
to bathe their children before bed,
time to water the garden.

He uncoils the hose, mists the poppies'
parchment lids half-closed to the loam
of their opiate pupils, sweeps the bowed

hem of Siberian iris. The rabbit's stone
forehead stipples, and its back drenches
to a deeper gray. From this chair,

I want to see the leaves recessing:
cosmos and violets self-sealed,
saving their blooms for truer darkness,

soon waking to a nightlife of weeds,
to leggy stalks of volunteers
prickling cracks in the cement border

while the wind stokes fireflies, stirring
bee strings from the recent hush
of this flashflood we only watched.

THE WATERCOLORS OF JOHN SINGER SARGENT:
A CATALOGUE

You can thumb through it
when the baby finally sleeps,
and you're craving two minutes
of elsewhere: bleached pilasters

to stripe the canal's noon mirror;
the Bedouin's sapphire turban,
his eyes' conundrum of jet and gleam—
no story line to interrupt,

but pages of women tumbled in the grass
like lilies spilled from a bushel;
girls aloft in their hoops,
lost under parasols: Happy Birthday,

here are the holidays we haven't had,
the retirement home I can still want:
a courtyard in summer,
where two friends guard

the leafy door to the unformed.
One studies violet light
and oak script. The wall clouds.
A book lies in her lap, unread.

WHEN:
ON A PAINTING BY CATHERINE McCARTHY

You lay in bed listening
to conversation in a bass clef.
No, sounds. Indian voices,
you thought: something
with a music in it
close enough to catch.

You were a child
hearing voices, seeding
this green seascape
and its burial mound
of words: *when*
become wind, become *W*—
one letter flourishes,
grandiloquent in upper case.

Now the lake is glaucous,
painted still. No light
could be this light.
And in the still of letters,
I am—writing anecdote
for you: small profile then,
waiting for shape
to evanesce and go again.

THE ANNUNCIATION,
ATTRIBUTED TO PETRUS CHRISTUS

In first silvering dawn you wake, one hand pressed
to your belly of weather, to its rise and swell
of hidden water. You shift in the sheets, your palm an ear
to the atmosphere the baby breathes (glass of ether,
glass of wine?) as mist settles the mint leaves

and lilies wild in the stone-rimmed heart
of your garden. By the wall crumbled low to the road,
a winged man walks, wing rustling pendant wing
as you move to your window—
morning's envelope waiting to be torn,

to be dappled open by words: *how poorly
flesh fits divinity,* you think. For you've expected
all of it: the swelling child, those cumbering wings,
the knock at your door and slow mouthful of stars
when the angel Gabriel speaks—

Thou art most blessed among women,
glass of ether, glass of wine:
you're a wife in flower and a girl intact,
an arid bud never watered by love. And as the angel
bows his head, his wings' lucent membrane

threads indigo and red: a dim underside of fireflies.
No, a rash of color stitched by a craftsman,
skeins jeweling rivers on his table.
The seam hovers close enough to touch—
but a light stills your hand. And now it's morning.

LADY'S SLIPPER

If the heart were pared
to two rose kidney-
chambers, furled
in the grass—

if cursive veins
scribbled at the seam
where the two halves
paled and interleaved—

if, on these thumbnail
tablets of instruction,
the letters bled
at the moment

I tried to read—
still the pines
would shelter
the soft graft,

never knowing
the sense of its stitch,
what words
weave a ventricle,

what serif
or arabesque
stains there
to plot a body's need.

MINIATURE

It was only an everyday betrayal.

But today your faithlessness
lives as a natural law,
clear as a mist-dimmed
mountain disrobing:

the brisk *I forgot;*
the fierce *I lost*—
lies you no longer know
you're telling. And lies

suit you: the mountain
morphs to shoreline;
your eyes take on
a planetary sheen...

now a family of mollusks
scatters.

You're becoming
a seascape
I want to brush
in miniature, fever

in an inch
of India ink—
then press in a locket
for unsentimental ends.

But one sea truth
is only half a locket.
It needs the twin oblong
of my tidal acquiescence,

burbled back
to sand-combed
and silt-glazed you—

the breathless
facing page of it! —

as if you've granted me
a lifelong dream
to co-write fiction:

the *it's so nice,* the *of course not,*
the *you didn't need to.*

BLUE

It's early still when dusk turns
its face to the wall of this hotel room,
and a man brings a woman to the edge
of a star-white bed, his legs

surrounding hers, his hands a mass
of brushstrokes on her waist, his clavicle
in shadow under the bluing eaves.
Now they only half-know

what they've waited for so long:
the bounty of hours; a night all hands,
all mouth. As he unhooks her long skirt,

her shoulder blades articulate, divide
the room into hollows; and he closes his eyes
and murmurs again in Spanish.

IRIS DIAPHRAGM

Wander in the iris swamp
until you find a blossom
wide as your palm,

complex as frisée.
Nip it. Now cup
its dusky whirlpools,

gauging their resistance.
Fold the petals,
taking care

not to fray the beard.
Roll gently.
Float this softened pencil

to your pinhole harbor,
where it unfurls
to brace

your inner stop.
House the brackets
that clamped thin air,

and they'll gird you
for the imminent
sounding: purple sepals

aproning your essence,
and one ore vein
to plate your raw

hutch. Trust the veil,
the unseen
breakwater:

failsafe;
to stem
an unfledged life.

HYDRANGEA

No other flower's such a stranger to soil.
Its curvature of blossom
turns a whelk, a fluid syllable
of seashell. For hydrangea is charged

with the stain of sea-change: no other flower
ripens as it dies, testing the slender range
of colors we can identify—

not red, not brown; hinterlands
between rose and violet. We grasp
as if through fog that liquid sense,
cast a root in the ocean floor: somewhere

deeper than we've ever been,
hydrangea waves muscular as coral,
shading starfish and silt.

REST

Jackson Pollock, 1951,
photograph by Hans Namuth

The parked Ford dappled like an arbor,
like a lake speaking in shallows, and Pollock
finally acquiesced: he sank to the running board
and rested his elbows on his knees,
let his bare head hang in the morning's balance.

Namuth watched him and considered:
If fire could slump...
while the light searched Pollock's folds for sparks,
appraising half his frown and a jean cuff,
then modeling his hands' flight from his lap,
a forgotten cigarette ringing ash.

Add a tree or mountain,
and Pollock might have looked out far,
his small form Hudson River-spry.
But this sky was white as the moment before movies,
and his eyes followed his fingers to the ground:

how aloof, those fingers; how open
and empty the car, with its battered door
and lure of unforgiving wheel.
How little, after all, he knew of the periphery.

BOOK OF DAYS

for my father
and in memory of John Fiorito

You'd meet him
in the wet seasons,

raking leaves,
pruning;

you compared
fertilizer, pondered
stocks—he'd come inside

for a glass of wine,
some firelight.

One November,
he knew he wouldn't see
Christmas:

before the hospital,
before the spasms,

he kept
his body's counsel:

no pain, no inkling
of a god—he just felt

his spleen shut, his
occiput shift.

Then he could see you

alone in the nut-brown
rack of your garden

in March,

your head bowed
to the parched forsythia,

and he provided you

a book of days

to find
under the evergreen
at Christmas—

he had already
written the card:

he wanted you
to laugh every evening;

he wanted you to grow
even older.

FIRST SEASON

Even in March,
you can sense
a shearing;
or spring's first skin
has molted:

the witch hazel's
gold spindles
now revert
to bracts,

and the flowering quince
has shed
its early blooms,
clearing baroque
tangles of branches;

look around you
carefully
for chrysalis, hoping
the season
hasn't spent;

and see the magnolia
still enfolded, all
electric in its buds—
fronting

the Scotch broom's
empty cloud:
such an early
discrete storm.

CROWN

And now it seems to me the beautiful uncut hair of graves.
—Walt Whitman

Not the waved
passage to my waist;
not the swath
lining
my nape—

not even the wide
brocade, sash
to wrap
a man in;
no, I miss

the weight
where it began,
the part hard-won
in the skull's
hive of roots: halo

or underbrush
ruffed between
my thoughts
and the atmosphere—

but *crowning glory*
fell from me, letter
by cursive
letter, each strand
slenderer

than thread,
draining
in wet heaps
when I washed,

then combed
until my bones
faltered
in the milkweed
trickle—

head of silver rushes
knotted
in back
when I died—

then they dressed me
paler still, sealed
my plot of hair,
winter grass
growing.

MOURNING CLOAK
(Nymphalis antiopa)

How it burdens, under glass:
the gray shingles of the wings
pressed from flight, slate
or wood grain
once thinned to buoyancy
when this butterfly
peppered streams,
its cloak hemmed
in near glint, grief
worn as lightness,
its crape wild
in the open air
between two sleeps.

III.

And therefore as a stranger give it welcome.
—William Shakespeare

GREAT LAKES

The Soul's Superior instants
Occur to Her—alone—
—Emily Dickinson

Chafe your hands
over my soul's
gas ring,

and you'll glean
the warmth there,
flickering;

but my coldness
is ample:
the bounty

of any bridle.
Copse and thicket,
arboring.

Or sunrise lake trills:
startle, re-startle—
swum.

Within a wedge
of darkness,
the burrowed

life resides,
perennial
novitiate:

good morning,
Lake Superior.

ON PATERNITY

To have a child,
you have to love the world enough
to show it to a stranger for the first time.
Or at least to witness that discovery:
watch the skittish fingers
clutch at petals; bear the piano noise,
soon to be a miracle of scales.

That is what I wasn't sure about.

I can't teach joy,
and the world won't show its splendor
to just anyone.
The greatest comforts are the easiest to miss:
the generosity of rain,
what sunrise makes of winter grass.

How to teach a child not to overlook?

Huddled creature, paralyzed—
take from me a scavenger's eye,
my concave soul unsuited to a wife,
and this hillside rolling out
indifference like a saving grace.

COLD SONG

to my sister

In Buffalo the snowflakes turn,
large as hands
shaken in the porch light.

The streets trace salt
under the moon.

On the night you were born,
I watched
my first movie—

the story of a governess
and edelweiss

*(may you bloom
and grow),*

while you lay
above the drifts
sloping the hospital yard:

furrowed in
from a closer night,

no shoot yet
fissuring the ice.

MIRROR STAGE

A welter of webs
before they were limbs,
your limbs—

and never sat
a belonging
there: from among

the daily
flinch and sputter,
an arm riddled,

splintered
to its fingered end—

lonely. The feel
of no one at the helm.

While foreign forces
moved you,
draping

your tentacles,
hex-legged and fluent
only in rivering—

nodding
like rings of monarchs
pinned above your crib,

or octopal
as the blown branch
honeying the window—

until the day
your hairless globe
stuns in the mirror:

sunspot
or manhole,
sweet dominion

over the two and two
and five
and five:

round governor
wrested
from liquidity,

dear as a sovereign
in your palm:

and now
the mirror mints
your stubborn head.

MORNING WITH THE MASSAGE THERAPIST

Sweet hub
of muscle,
glazed face:

offer yourself
in clothes each day
to the world;

sand your life
to the quick. You,
who want to be

furniture,
kiln-roared
earthenware,

this morning are
a candidate
for waterways:

ten firm
fingers
on one rib.

Tears well up
from a shoulder—
you're Venice.

From a thigh—
Texas oil fields.
Now the terrible bridge

your neck is:
the roiling songs
of ocean in your ears,

a sick rip
of continents,
your stomach

wracked
to break your fall,
and you'll splay

dumb in your own
salt water, dupe
of tides.

SAVIOR

Guido Reni, *Saint Sebastian* (ca. 1630)

Then, Sebastian:
torso phosphorescent
as gills upturned
in foaming light—

his waist white as rabies,
as crusted tundra
and snow mass, the roped
loincloth loosened

from his hips,
and an arrow grown
in the hub of shadow
pooled beneath his rib.

Here, no strung beads,
no bloodstream to clot;
but the pearled husk
passes for a boy's depth:

a smitten God
preserves those sinews
like fossils, trussing
the divine hide—

and infection's exiled
to the waters he's risen from:
pierced and wrung, rinsed
in an afterbirth of storms.

DIAGRAMMATIC

What is the soul of a sentence?

Can we diagram it
in the ancient way?

Does it climb a rack of syntax,
figure-eight in barbed wire,

or whorl into stops
and variants of stops:

periods,
the air-strung colon,
a comma's glissade?

Perhaps it flocks
to a word like *isinglass*
or puckers in *absinthe*—

burrows in vocabulary
knotted with cedar
and lungwort.

Does the sentence's soul
resemble us?

Can it animate our smoke,
our second-hand?

Or does it carve
the stratus face
God turns to us daily,

cradled in the crook
of his arm—

brief incandescent
wedge—

before he snuffs the firmament
we waver against,
back-lit?

THE BLIND POEM

If you line your heart with it,
you're settling for metaphor.

You must build a home for it,
but neither wood nor brick.

It needs a soft ceiling:
one feather or a swath

of rabbit fur. Mummify it.
Wind it in the ripple-pools

of marble Hellenistic folds;
make a miser's tabernacle,

parchment yellowing.
It will never know a reader's eye:

the universe, to a poem.
Blinded, it belongs to you.

ENCEINTE

I need to trust them,
the young
married couple
on the bus
each morning,

the husband's
right arm
always walling
her face
in muscle,

capturing
her beacon smile
spanning
moonless plashes
every day;

like a postulant,
I'll believe
his counter-smile's
a realized
intransitive,

a strain of love
tough enough
to breed:
I believe
love is natural

for some. Others
lick eyebright,
study fingering,
or weave
a pair

of unseen skins
at night: imagine
how his back,
imprinting
tributaries,

shades the place
her gathered
hair fans—bolts
of rusted silk,
the ease of lightning.

PILAR

Five days I baked
in Denver, she said.
Laid my body out,
burnt it brown.

My dress was black.
Backless.
One earlobe
bitten raw.

That's how I looked
when I drove to Pilar,
she said,
pit stop
on the low road

to Santa Fe,
bits of clay and sticks
littering the banks
of the Rio Grande.

I knew he worked the rafts all day.
Five dollars an hour,
tips sometimes
from tourists.

When he saw me,
he almost smiled.
Took me to his trailer
to smoke some weed,
fucked me on the stinking grass.

He didn't say
a word, she said.
Didn't have to.
I heard my beauty
chatter in the wind.

LISTS

The trouble with us
is *if I didn't,*
if I had, the *if I had*
children,
the way we

unmoor ourselves
from tasks
so our bodies
somehow sink
in the horizon,

radiate like East
River sunsets,
our cells lifting
and scattering
in landfills,

as if we toy
with *limitless*
just to comb
the world
of ourselves: so if

we're washing linens,
a sheet might peak
like a sail
in the cycle,
a soft jet's wing

that beckons
us to list
with *If I didn't,*
if I didn't work—
if I never came home

but was home
always, how
would my hands
define the oak
table? Would I say

It's quiet here,
*it's quiet...*or if I never
came home,
how would I remember
my four walls,

could I sand
my mind
of everything
but one pale curl
of paint peeling?

Remember the critic
who said with a smile,
No, I'm not
black, but I could
have been,

I could have:
the trouble with us
is still the shock
of being
in our skins at all.

IMITATIONS

after Fannie Hurst's *Imitation of Life*, 1933

I stop there, for who can tell me what beauty is?
—Frantz Fanon, *Black Skin, White Masks*

Bea Pullman.

Delilah was my first.
Before her, I couldn't afford servants—
I whirled from the kitchen
to the bath,
burning eggs on the stove
while my baby splashed
and laughed with her rubber duck
and cried in earnest.
Delilah took pity
and moved in.
She cooked for me,
she and her light brown daughter.

I guess a woman could do worse
than pan for gold on a griddle.
When my lawyer friend whispered,
"Box the flour,"
I caught my breath:
a pancake empire—
hailstorms of coins, those
pennies from heaven.

We nailed Delilah's face
to the sign, lit her neon
kerchief in the night.
Negro beacon
of a secret flour,
the tattoo of her hard smile
gathered mouths
from everywhere,

and the hail fell.

Peola Johnson.

She wore suits,
high heels,
a stiff satin brim
to cameo her face.
At night, a line of sequins
bordered her shoulders,
scooped from her clavicle.

I'd climb the stairs halfway
and watch the dancers
list beneath the chandeliers.
Rice powder and rouge,
lips cranberried:
I looked at Miss Bea Pullman
and told myself,
that's a face I could wear.

I don't look like my mother.
She might not be
my mother at all:
little girl Moses
I could have been,
dappled helpless
in the rushes,
then pressed
to the lumpen creases
of a black body
welling love like tears,
blessing me
with a lifetime ticket
on the Jim Crow car.

Delilah Johnson.

"We ain't born dumb, Miss Bea,"
I told her. "We gets that way later."
Happen to me, I swear.
Happen to me, now my girl
ain't my girl no more—

smartest in the schoolroom
she was, little head
behind the book,
little angel, she leave me—
Miss Bea say she *disavow* me.

Now a uppity cashier
in the white man's hotel,
New York City,
cheerful as you please.
I go to her, hold out my hand,
and she turn her face
away. Say, "I never see
this woman before
in my life."

In my life.
Words they fell me,
tree-like. Lay my head
on the cool counter,
cover my eyes—
see myself lay out in roses.
No, th'other ones, can't
remember the name—
blossom sound like *Peola.*

MARCH IN NEW YORK

Again today, a mourning dove
waits in the fir branch
outside my window
in Staten Island.

She's so close
I can see her blink
at raindrops, as water
pours from the curb
in currents: at last,
near-flood after drought.

After September,
I'd like to call it *washing*.
I'd like to say *immersion*.

The dove has stayed for days.
Yesterday she hovered,
and I saw the flat
thatch of sticks beneath her—
a loose weave
among the needles.

And then the baby's beak
pointing up from that shifting floor,
covered again
when the mother returned
to brood
over latticework

and wings—but modestly,
unthinking. Of course,
I thought. As one gives birth
unthinking. As one gives birth,
nowadays, regardless.

AMARYLLIS

Thus we can at least observe a purposiveness according to form, without basing it on a purpose....
—Immanuel Kant, *Critique of Judgment*

Eight blossoms from a single bulb:
it is prolific as certain mothers,
as authors worth the salt of their authority.

From one green trunk of stem,
four flowers rise to separate music:
red petals whorl and blister,

whitening their centers,
framing seven stamens arched
to the stained tips of their pollen sacs.

When the weight of these four blossoms
sways the stem, we'll stake it up,
bandage it with raffia,

and watch another nibbed stalk
doubling from the bulb—
while coruscated older petals

thirst into husk,
toughened to transparency
in pleats of levied veins

correlate with dust:
purposiveness, economy
the world can't use or live without.

PALIMPSEST

This is the way
stars die in the city:
the shroud
of our windows' light
lifts like the sea

of sky in California,
the night
a rant of glint
pressed my spine
to the grass,

floating me
in the navy
sleeping bag
I had grown
only halfway into.

Still blind to pattern
and metaphor,
I dipped my face
to the dark, cracked
that vastest

book of stars,
and exhaled, tracing
alphabets. Now
even a blanching sky
returns me

to a home
before doors:
frontispiece
of harp and hunter,
jewels legible on black.

Christina Pugh is the author of *Gardening at Dusk*, a chapbook of poems published by Wells College Press. She has received a Ruth Lilly Poetry Fellowship from *Poetry* magazine, the Grolier Poetry Prize, the Associated Writing Programs' Intro Award in Poetry, a Whiting Fellowship for the Humanities, and three nominations for a Pushcart Prize, among other honors. Her poems have recently appeared in *The Atlantic Monthly*, *Ploughshares*, *Columbia: A Journal of Literature and Art*, *Poetry Daily*, and in the anthology *Poetry 180: A Turning Back to Poetry*. She holds degrees from Wesleyan University, Harvard University, and Emerson College, and is currently visiting assistant professor of English at Northwestern University.

Printed in the United States
20050LVS00001B/180

9 781932 339345